Changing Our Community

Ben Nussbaum

Reader Consultants

Jennifer M. Lopez, M.S.Ed., NBCT
Senior Coordinator—History/Social Studies
Norfolk Public Schools

Tina Ristau, M.A., SLMS
Teacher Librarian
Waterloo Community School District

iCivics Consultants

Emma Humphries, Ph.D.
Chief Education Officer

Taylor Davis, M.T.
Director of Curriculum and Content

Natacha Scott, MAT
Director of Educator Engagement

Publishing Credits

Rachelle Cracchiolo, M.S.Ed., *Publisher*
Emily R. Smith, M.A.Ed., *VP of Content Development*
Véronique Bos, *Creative Director*
Dona Herweck Rice, *Senior Content Manager*
Dani Neiley, *Associate Content Specialist*
Fabiola Sepulveda, *Series Designer*

Image Credits: p10 vewfinder/Shutterstock; p12 stock_photo_world/Shutterstock; p13 VineStar/Shutterstock; p14 Flickr/KOMUnews; pp.16-17, 25 US Department of Education; p24 milehightraveler/iStock; all other images from iStock and/or Shutterstock

Library of Congress Cataloging-in-Publication Data

Names: Nussbaum, Ben, 1975- author.
Title: Changing our community / Ben Nussbaum.
Description: Huntington Beach, CA : Teacher Created Materials, [2021] | Includes index. | Audience: Grades 2-3 | Summary: "Communities are always changing. Streets get fixed. Sidewalks get added. New schools get built. But how does it all happen?"-- Provided by publisher.
Identifiers: LCCN 2020043566 (print) | LCCN 2020043567 (ebook) | ISBN 9781087604985 (paperback) | ISBN 9781087620008 (ebook)
Subjects: LCSH: Social change--Juvenile literature. | Political participation--Juvenile literature. | Civic improvement--Juvenile literature.
Classification: LCC HM831 .N87 2021 (print) | LCC HM831 (ebook) | DDC 303.4--dc23
LC record available at https://lccn.loc.gov/2020043566
LC ebook record available at https://lccn.loc.gov/2020043567

TCM Teacher Created Materials
5482 Argosy Avenue
Huntington Beach, CA 92649-1039
www.tcmpub.com

ISBN 978-1-0876-0498-5

Table of Contents

Changing All the Time

Change is everywhere. It is in big cities. It is in small towns. But it is not always easy. Making changes to **communities** takes a lot of work. It takes planning. Many people must work together to figure out which changes should be made. But how do these **decisions** get made?

Many Communities

A community can be a group of people who live in the same area. But it can also be a group of people who share some beliefs or do the same thing, such as playing a sport.

Jump into Fiction

Speaking Up

"Why do we need to spend money to build a new school? Can't it just be repaired?" Amy heard someone ask. A lot of people were at the town council meeting. They wanted to give their opinions on the new school.

Amy leaned over to her mom. "Am I allowed to say something?"

"Of course! This is your school. Let them know what you think," her mom said.

Amy took a breath and stood up. "It is not enough just to do repairs. The buildings are too small. There are so many kids now. The new school could have bigger rooms and better science labs. It's important for us and for future kids." People clapped as she sat down.

The next week, Mr. Wilson spoke to the class.

"I have some good news to share," he said. "A lot of you know that there has been talk about building a new school. Amy, I even heard you speak at the meeting last week," he added.

"Well, I'm happy to share that the vote is in. We are getting a new school!"

Amy smiled. She was glad that she spoke up and proud that she helped others make this decision.

Back to Nonfiction

A Lot to Think About

Sometimes, communities want to make changes. Maybe a street needs to be paved. Maybe an old building is falling apart and a new one needs to be built.

Community workers repave a street.

Before a change can happen, there is a lot to think about. People have to ask questions and **brainstorm**. What will it cost? Will it cause problems? How long will it take? Are there other **solutions**?

A citizen speaks at a local meeting.

Vote for Change

When a community needs to make a decision, it can ask for help. Sometimes, it needs help from the community members. Maybe a town wants to add a new crosswalk. There might be people who think this is a good idea. Others might think it will cause traffic problems. The town can have a meeting. People can go and **debate**. They can **vote** for the changes they want.

Voting

Voting is great way to make a difference. When you vote, you share your opinion. Once people have talked and brainstormed, a vote is a good way to make the final decision.

These students vote for class president.

A Big Change

Other issues need more work. For example, building a school is a big change. Maybe a town is growing. A new school could make a big difference. But it is **expensive**. People in the community have to pay for it with **taxes**.

A town has to decide if it makes sense to spend the money on a school. The people have to talk. They have to find the best plan for everyone.

A teacher talks to members of a school board.

Helpful Taxes

Taxes help pay for more than just big changes, such as new schools. They help pay for things such as trash collection or fixing roads.

What Is Best?

Some people might like the town the way it is. They may not want a new school. Building a school costs a lot of money. It could take a long time. Some people might not think it is the best idea.

Leaders share their ideas in a town meeting.

So, both sides can vote for leaders who support their views. Choosing good leaders who represent them is important. It is one way for people to affect how their communities change.

Many Voices

Leaders aren't the only ones who can help. Community members can also help make change happen. They can send letters, make phone calls, go to local meetings, or vote. They can talk to the leaders. But a lot of people have to help. Many voices are louder than one voice. Working together is a good way to make change. It helps get things done!

People sign up to vote.

Think and Talk

How are people in these photos helping to make change in their communities?

What Now?

What happens if a school needs to close? There might not be enough kids to fill the school anymore. The community has to decide what to do.

People have to ask questions. Should a small town keep its own school? Or should nearby towns share one big school? The community has to think about what will be best. It is a difficult choice that some small towns have to make.

A One-Room School

Children of all ages used to be in the same room at school. Schools had just one room for all the students to learn together.

If a school closes, does it mean the debate is over? No. The town has to decide what to do next. Maybe some people want to tear down the building. Maybe others want to turn it into a library. The town must talk again. Remember, change is everywhere. So, a decision made one day might change in the future!

A student makes a speech about changes she thinks are needed.

People debate the change they want to make.

Help Make Change

Communities are always changing. They might create new parks. They might build shopping centers. It is good to remember that each person in a community can be part of the change.

City officials cut a ribbon at a new train station.

A woman shares her ideas at a community meeting.

Wherever you live, you can help make it better. Write to your leaders. Go to a meeting. Ask others to help. Speak up! It is your community. You can help make a change!

Glossary

brainstorm—to think of different ideas

communities—groups of people who are connected to one another

debate—to talk about something with people who have different opinions

decisions—the results of making choices

expensive—costing a lot of money

solutions—answers to problems

taxes—money collected by the government to pay for things used by the public

vote—to make an official choice for a person or an idea

Index

Civics in Action

To be heard, you have to speak up! Let your thoughts be known. You can share them with your community leaders right now.

1. Get the names and office addresses or emails of the leaders in your community.

2. Think about a problem in your community or something you think is really great.

3. Write a letter or email to your local leaders. Tell them your thoughts and what you think should be done.

4. Thank them for taking your thoughts into consideration. Be sure to sign your name!

5. Send them your letter or email.